ASK A
SHARK AND OTHER SEA CREATURES

olivia Brookes

PowerKiDS press
New York

Published in 2009 by The Rosen Publishing Group, Inc.
29 East 21st Street, New York, NY 10010

Copyright © 2009 Orpheus Books Ltd

All rights reserved. No part of this book may be reproduced in any form without permission in writing from the publisher, except by a reviewer.

Created and produced by: Julia Bruce, Rachel Coombs, Nicholas Harris, Sarah Hartley, and Erica Simms, Orpheus Books Ltd

Text: Olivia Brookes

U.S. editor: Kara Murray

Illustrated by: Ian Jackson (*The Art Agency*)

Consultant: Kathie Way, The Natural History Museum, London.

Library of Congress Cataloging-in-Publication Data

Brookes, Olivia.
A shark and other sea creatures / Olivia Brookes. —
1st ed.
p. cm. — (Ask)
Includes index.
ISBN 978-1-4358-2515-4 (library binding)
1. Marine animals—Juvenile literature. I. Title.
QL122.2.B76 2009
591.77—dc22
2008005826

Manufactured in China

contents

4 Do Sharks Eat Humans?

6 What Is It Like to Be a Marine Creature?

8 What Does an Octopus Use Its Arms For?

10 Which Animals Live on a Coral Reef?

12 How Do Fish Defend Themselves?

14 Why Do Turtles Swim Long Distances?

16 Who Lives in the Kelp Forest?

18 What Do Manatees Do All Day?

20 Why Do Dolphins Play and Leap?

22 What Do Humpback Whales Eat?

24 How Does a Penguin Survive the Cold?

26 How Far Does an Albatross Fly?

28 Which Sea Creatures Glow?

30 Who Lives at the Bottom of the Ocean?

32 Glossary, Index, and Web Sites

Introduction

Welcome to the world's oceans. Water covers 70 percent of our planet, and the seas and oceans are filled with life. There are millions of creatures that live here—in, on, or above the water. We'd like to tell you what our lives are like, so ask us questions and we'll do our best to answer you. Maybe you'd like to know where the manatee lives? Or which animals can live at the very bottom of the ocean where it is freezing cold, pitch-black, and completely silent? The parrotfish will tell you what life is like on a coral reef, the green turtle explains why she swims thousands of miles (km) across the Atlantic Ocean to lay her eggs, while the albatross describes what it's like to fly around the world. First, you will hear from one of the scariest creatures in the ocean, the great white shark.

Do Sharks Eat Humans?

We sharks are best known for our sudden attacks on humans. And it's true, we are dangerous. We kill about 16 people every year.

I am a great white shark. I'm big, fast, and very strong. I have razor-sharp teeth and a good sense of smell, thousands of times better than yours.

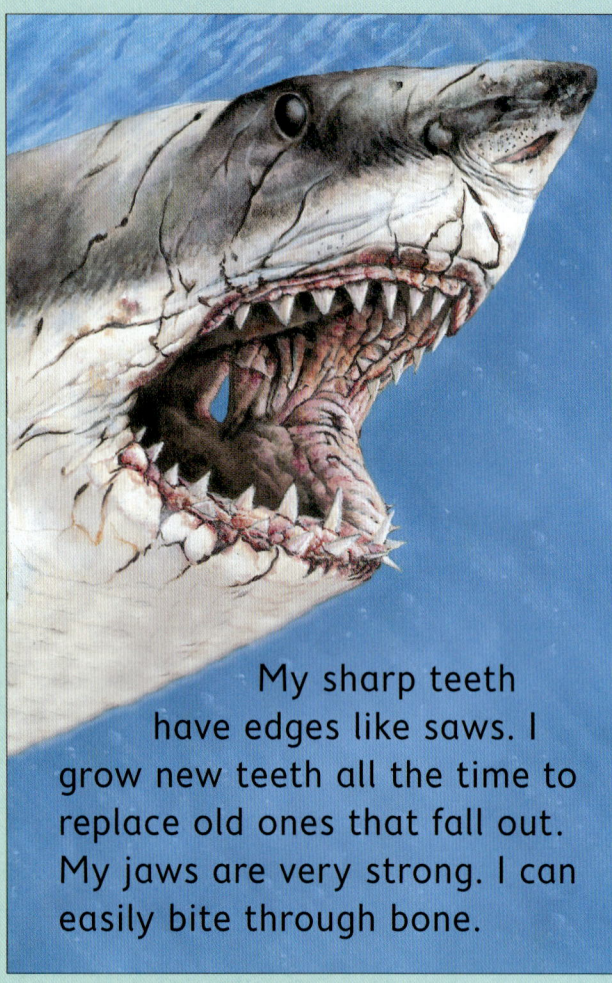

My sharp teeth have edges like saws. I grow new teeth all the time to replace old ones that fall out. My jaws are very strong. I can easily bite through bone.

To us sharks, you humans look like seals or other big sea animals when you swim.

Sometimes we are curious and take a bite out of a human, but we don't like the way you taste. You don't have enough fat. We like seals much better.

My skeleton isn't made of bone. It's made of a flexible material called cartilage, the same stuff your ears are made of.

I can whip around in a second to catch my prey by surprise. I'm a fast swimmer, too, much faster than you are.

I normally eat fish and sea mammals, such as seals and porpoises. I can leap out of the water to grab my prey in midair.

This is a tiger shark, a close relative of mine. He can grow up to 20 feet (6 m) long. He is very dangerous to you humans because he will eat almost anything. He swims very close to the water's surface looking for his prey.

Check out the weird shape of this hammerhead. It can see better with its eyes like that.

What is it Like to Be a Marine Creature?

I am a sea anemone. I might look pretty, but I'm a predator. Those tentacles around my mouth have deadly stingers.

I live on rocks in shallow pools. When danger comes, I can flatten myself against the rocks.

I am a sea urchin. I spend my life eating algae, or tiny plants, on the seabed. Inside my spiny shell I'm really just a stomach with a mouth at the bottom and a bottom at the top.

We lobsters live busy lives. I crawl along the sea bed in shallow water, hide in rock piles, catch shrimp, and dig for clams and urchins with my strong claws. My body has a hard shell that can't grow. When it gets too small, I molt, or shed, my shell. A new one hardens in its place.

There are a huge number of different marine creatures living in the sea. I'm a starfish. I have a shell inside my body. My mouth is on my belly.

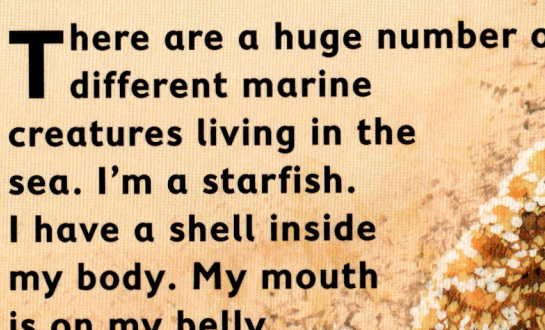

After I open these mussels with my feet, I push my stomach into the shells to eat what's inside.

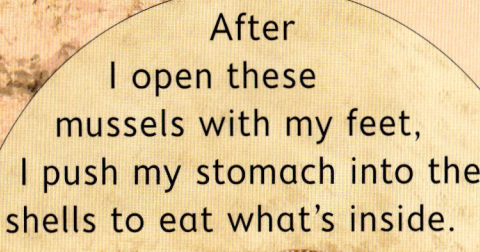

We scallops have two shells joined together at a hinge. We move around by closing our shells quickly to force water, pushing us forward.

I am a sea slug. I eat sea anemones and I store their stingers on my back to use as a weapon.

We are a Portuguese man-of-war. We're not a single animal, but lots of small ones joined together. Some of us sting prey while others eat them.

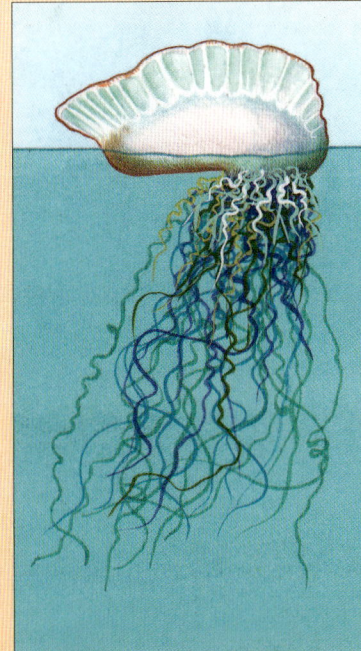

What Does an Octopus Use Its Arms For?

I am a red octopus. I live in the Pacific Ocean. You'll find octopuses big and small in all the world's seas and oceans.

This is a close-up of my eyeball. Octopus eyes are the sharpest of any invertebrate, or an animal without a backbone. Like you, we can see in color. Most other sea creatures can't. Color is very important to us. We can quickly change the color of our skin to match what's around us. Our colors get brighter when we are surprised or scared.

My body is soft with no bones or shell. My brain is the biggest of any invertebrate. I have eight strong arms. I use them to fight, grab things, and move about. Each arm has rows of suckers. These help me to catch fish and crabs to eat.

The suckers on my arms give me an excellent grip on this tasty crab.

You'll find my mouth in the center of my body. I have a hard, sharp beak like a parrot's and a rough tongue. I can also spit poison.

We octopuses only live for a year or two. We only have babies once in our lives. When they hatch, our babies drift with the sea currents. Many get eaten before they can grow into adults.

When I'm trying to escape from a predator, I squirt clouds of black ink into the water. This confuses my attacker and gives me a chance to get away. I suck water into my body, then squirt it out quickly. This pushes me to safety!

Which Animals Live on a Coral Reef?

I am a coral polyp. I'm just a tiny fraction of an inch (cm) across. Those wavy tentacles catch my food for me. At my base, I have a hard skeleton.

Coral reefs are home to many sea creatures like me, a whitetip reef shark. Coral only grows in clear, warm, shallow water. The sea here on the Great Barrier Reef, off the northeast coast of Australia, is perfect! Reefs are made from the skeletons of millions of coral polyps. Tiny plants, called algae, grow on the coral. They give them their bright colors. They also supply the goodness that the coral polyps need to build their skeletons.

We giant sponges look like long tubes, but we are animals, too. Water passes through tiny holes in our bodies. We digest tiny pieces of food in the water.

I'm a parrotfish. I eat coral with my hard, beaked mouth. But that crown-of-thorns starfish is a bigger threat to the reef. It eats live coral. When the coral dies, the reef dies.

I'm a sea horse. Like these angelfish here, I hide in the reef when danger comes. See that whitetip shark looking for a meal? Predators like that sneak up on us if we're not careful. I have to watch that moray eel over there, too.

How do Fish Defend Themselves?

We fish have found lots of clever ways of not being eaten. I'm a stonefish, the most poisonous fish in the world.

Porcupine fish, like me, have three lines of defense. I am usually small and harmless. But if there's danger, I swallow water and swell to more than twice my size. Sharp spines stick out all over my body. I'm also poisonous!

I'm a cowfish. We are also called boxfish because of our square shape. My body is protected by a hard cover made of stiff plates. I have sharp horns on my head and tail. When I am scared, my skin also makes a deadly poison.

I am a clown fish. The anemones' poisonous tentacles protect me from enemies, but don't hurt me at all.

Flying fish escape from predators by swimming very fast, then leaping out of the water. We glide above the surface on our winglike fins. When we splash down again, the danger, usually a tuna or swordfish, is far behind us.

We mullets have silvery scales that reflect light. When we swim together, the flash is blinding.

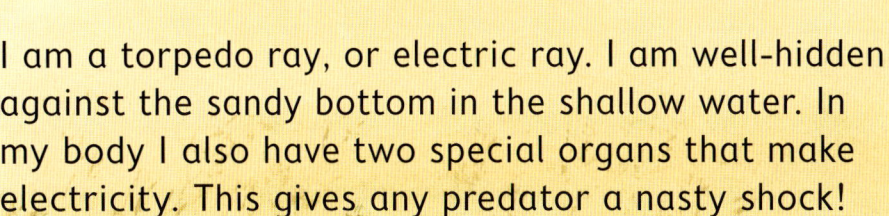

I am a young angelfish. I confuse predators with the eyelike markings near my tail. They attack the wrong end of my body and give me a chance to escape.

I spend all my time on the sea bed. I am well camouflaged, so I usually just hide from predators. But if I sense danger, I raise the poisonous spines running down my back.

I am a torpedo ray, or electric ray. I am well-hidden against the sandy bottom in the shallow water. In my body I also have two special organs that make electricity. This gives any predator a nasty shock!

Why Do Turtles Swim Long Distances?

I swim more than 1,000 miles (1,609 km) to the tiny island of Ascension, in the Atlantic Ocean, to lay my eggs.

AFRICA

ATLANTIC OCEAN

BRAZIL

Ascension Island

The island has no animals that might steal my eggs, so it's a perfect place for me to breed.

Green turtles, like me, live in the tropical oceans of the world. We spend most of our lives in our home waters, close to the coast. But every few years, we make long journeys, called migrations, to our breeding grounds to lay our eggs.

Our bodies are perfectly shaped for life underwater. Our shells are light and we have strong flippers. We can swim faster than you can ride a bicycle! We come up for air every few minutes when we swim, but we can hold our breath underwater for up to two hours while we sleep.

I come back to the same beach on Ascension Island where I was born. I lay about 100 eggs in a hole I dig in the sand. Then I cover them and return to the sea.

When we are babies, we eat seaweed, jellyfish, and shrimp. When we grow up, we only eat plants. This sea grass is delicious! We can grow to well over 3 feet (91 cm) long and can live for 80 years or more.

In two or three months, my eggs will hatch. The babies dig themselves out of the nest and head straight for the sea. Only one or two hatchlings out of every 100 live on.

Who Lives in the Kelp Forest?

I am a sea otter. This kelp forest, where I live, is off the west coast of North America. Kelp is a type of giant seaweed. It can grow to over 100 feet (30 m) high. That's taller than most trees. Lots of creatures live here, including sea urchins. These eat the kelp and could destroy it if they ate too much. Luckily, I eat sea urchins myself.

That's a sea urchin in my paw.

Sea urchins are spiny and hard to open. So first, I wrap them up in kelp to protect my paws. Then I crack them open on a stone that I put on my tummy. I eat shellfish this way, too.

Here's one of those nasty urchins up close. That sheepshead fish is one of the urchin's predators. Sheepsheads have strong, bony mouths that are great for crunching through tough shells. Did you know that they are all born female, and they turn into males when they get older?

Kelp grows really quickly, up to 20 inches (51 cm) a day. It fixes itself to the sea floor with a clawlike foot, called a holdfast. Then it grows up toward the sunlight. It doesn't need roots because it soaks up its vitamins straight from seawater. It grows best in cool water. We sea otters don't have a layer of blubber under our skin to keep us warm like seals and sea lions do. But our fur traps air bubbles and heat. Our fur is so thick that our skin never gets wet.

Seals and sea lions love to hunt fish, like these garibaldis, in the kelp forest.

Before I go to sleep, I wrap myself up in kelp leaves so I don't drift out to sea. We otters spend half the days sleeping or resting in a group called a raft.

What Do Manatees Do All Day?

We manatees are mammals who spend all our lives in the water. But we are actually related to elephants! Manatees live off the coast of Florida, around the islands of the West Indies, and off the coast of West Africa. We like warm water, so we all live in tropical areas. There are also manatees in the Amazon River in South America. They are smaller than we are and very rare.

This is me holding some plants with my flippers. I spend most of the day eating water plants. But I can also reach out of the water, or even pull myself ashore, to grab a juicy land plant. I have to come to the surface every few minutes to breathe.

Here I'm pulling up some sea grass with my lips. I have grinding teeth, called molars, to chew with. These teeth fall out when they get worn down, but new ones soon grow back.

We are very good swimmers and we love to play games. We especially like to play follow-the-leader.

We often rub against each other and sometimes kiss by touching noses. Mothers and babies, called calves, talk by whistling and squealing at each other. A baby will stay with its mother for two years.

A lot of things, like algae and tiny shellfish, called barnacles, grow on my skin. It feels good to scratch them off!

Why Do Dolphins Play and Leap?

I'm a mammal, so I have to breathe air. When I swim, I often come up to the surface to breathe through the blowhole on top of my head.

Boats are so much fun! We love to play and swim alongside them.

We dusky dolphins live in shallow seas near New Zealand, South Africa, and South America. We live in groups, called pods, sometimes with 1,000 or more dolphins. We leap out of the water to save energy when we swim. It's easier to move through air than water.

The markings on our bodies camouflage us. From above, we look like light reflecting off the water. Seen from below, our white bellies blend in with light from the sky.

Our bodies have the perfect, sleek shape for swimming fast. We swim by moving our powerful tail, called a fluke, up and down. We use our fins to steer and slow us down.

We herd fish together by slapping our fins on the water to scare them. They are easy to catch.

We love to leap and jump. We do amazing twists and backflips. This isn't just for fun. It also helps us clean our fins and tail by shaking off small marine parasites.

Look out! These tall fins belong to killer whales, our main predator. To escape, we rely on our speed and our ability to leap. Sometimes we can hear killer whales by sonar and make our escape before they find us.

To make our way in the dark ocean, we send out high-pitched noises and listen to their echoes when they bounce back from objects nearby. This is called sonar.

What Do Humpback Whales Eat?

This is me spy-hopping. I poke my head above the water and take a good look around before sliding back under.

I am a humpback whale, one of the biggest creatures in the world. We grow to more than 50 feet (15 m) long. You'll find us swimming in all the world's oceans.

This is krill, my favorite food.

We eat small fish and tiny shrimp called krill. We need to eat millions of krill every day. We have bristly plates, like teeth, called baleen, in our mouths.

We drink mouthfuls of water full of krill and fish. When we squirt the water out again through the baleen, food catches there.

When I leap into the air, it's called breaching. I land back in the water with a big splash. This tells other whales I'm here and also knocks parasites off my skin. Those grooves on my underside let my throat expand when I'm eating.

We have the biggest flippers of any whale. Our tails are huge, too. Mine is over 12 feet (3.7 m) wide. Barnacles and whale lice cling onto my body.

We breathe through two blowholes on top of our heads. At the surface, we spout spray high in the air. After a few quick breaths, we close our blowholes and dive down again.

We are called humpback whales because our backs curve when we dive. While we're under water, we talk to other whales in clicks and groans. Males also sing very beautiful, long mating songs.

How Does a Penguin Survive the Cold?

I am a king penguin. I live on islands near Antarctica, one of the coldest places on Earth. We live in large groups called colonies. We are the second-largest penguins in the world, after the emperor penguin.

1 My egg was laid in the summer. My mom then went off to find food, leaving my dad to keep me warm. He balanced my egg on his feet so it didn't touch the cold ground. He covered it with a warm, feathery flap between his legs. After a month, I hatched.

We are more at home in the water than on land. Our shape helps us move smoothly through the water, using our strong flippers.

2 I am covered in soft, black down. Mom and Dad still carry me on their feet. They feed me fish and squid, which they eat first and then spit up for me. I need to build up a layer of fat to keep warm.

We penguins have more feathers than any other bird. Down feathers close to our skin trap air and keep us warm. The top feathers are smooth and stiff to keep out the cold wind. Natural oil in our bodies spreads over our feathers to keep water out.

3 I'm two months old now. I've grown a thick covering of brown feathers. These keep me warm. My parents leave me with other chicks while they hunt.

4 Now that I'm ten months old, my adult feathers are coming through. I have built up a thick layer of blubber to keep me warm. It is also a food store. I can go without food for weeks at a time.

This is our colony. There are hundreds of thousands of us here on this icy, faraway island. It can be hard to find your mate in this huge crowd. So we all sing our own individual songs to find each other.

Our main predators when we are grown up are the leopard seal, fur seal, and killer whale.

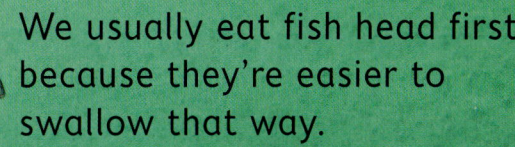

We usually eat fish head first because they're easier to swallow that way.

We can dive down deep for fish, our main food. We can stay under water for over seven minutes. Sometimes we leap right out of the water to breathe.

How Far Does an Albatross Fly?

When we are about seven years old, we start looking for mate. We do special courtship dances. It's very important to do this dance correctly, or we might not find a mate that year. Once we are paired up, though, it's for life.

I am a wandering albatross. I was born on South Georgia, an island near Antarctica. I go back there every other year to breed. But I spend most of my life gliding in the skies above the Southern Ocean. I go for months, even years, without touching land. In my lifetime, I'll fly around the world many times.

We build our nests from mud and grass. We lay just one egg at a time in winter. Both parents take turns sitting on the nest. After three months, it hatches.

I eat squid, octopus, and fish. I fly low over the water's surface to scoop them up. Sometimes I eat so much I can't fly! I have to rest on the sea until my tummy is empty. To feed my chicks, I spit up food I've eaten myself.

My strong, hooked beak is perfect for catching prey. I also have large nostrils on the top of my beak that help me smell food in the open ocean. We are sometimes called tubenoses because of these nostrils.

We are the largest kind of albatross. My wings are almost 12 feet (3.7 m) wide from tip to tip. That's the biggest wingspan of any bird in the world. My wings are narrow and stiff like a plane. I can fly for hours on air currents without flapping them once.

We follow ships, like this one, for days. Fishing boats often use lines with bait on hooks to catch tuna and swordfish. But it's dangerous to go after this bait. Many of us drown each year after getting caught on a hook.

Which Sea Creatures Glow?

We are sea creatures who live deep in the ocean. Sunlight doesn't reach this far down. Many of us create our own light with chemicals inside our bodies. It helps us to catch our prey and find our mate.

I am a viperfish. I have a special light organ at the end of a spine on my back. I hang it in front of my mouth and grab the prey as it comes near.

The shining bait on my head gives me my name, anglerfish. It's just like the bait on the end of a fishing rod. Other fish think it's food, but when they get close, I snap my jaws shut on them.

We are called lantern fish because of the light-making spots on our bellies.

I'm a hatchetfish. I am very thin and hard to see unless you're looking at me from the side.

I am only 3 inches (8 cm) long, but I can still cause trouble for my prey. I am a firefly squid. The tips of my tentacles have light-making parts. I flash these on and off to attract small fish. Then I grab them with my strong tentacles. My whole body can light up to attract a mate or confuse a predator.

I am a loosejaw. I can push my bottom jaw far out in front of me to catch prey. When I want to hide in the dark, I can also turn off the "headlights" under my eyes.

I am a gulper eel. My jaw is so big that I can actually swallow animals that are bigger than I am. I use the light organ on my tail to attract my victims. I can grow up to 6 feet (1.8 m) long, so you'd better watch out!

Even the tiniest creatures in the ocean can make light. We are zooplankton, microscopic animals that live in the water. It's really something when we glow in the dark. It looks like the water itself is glowing.

29

Who Lives at the Bottom of the Ocean?

Welcome to the bottom of the ocean! We are almost 3 miles (5 km) below the surface. It's dark, freezing cold, and silent. Creatures here use touch and smell, rather than sight and hearing, to find their way around. I am a grenadier, or rat-tail, fish. I swim along the ocean floor looking for food. My eyes help me see when I go up into shallower water.

My long, thin tail helps me find my prey in the dark. A special sensor running down my spine feels the movements of other creatures nearby.

I'm a tripodfish. I'm resting on the ocean floor on my three stiff fins. I have two other special fins that I wave over my head like ears. These help me find prey.

I am an umbrella sea pen. Like a lot of things that live in the dark, I am completely white.

We are Venus flower basket sponges.

We sea cucumbers suck up bits of dead animals and plants.

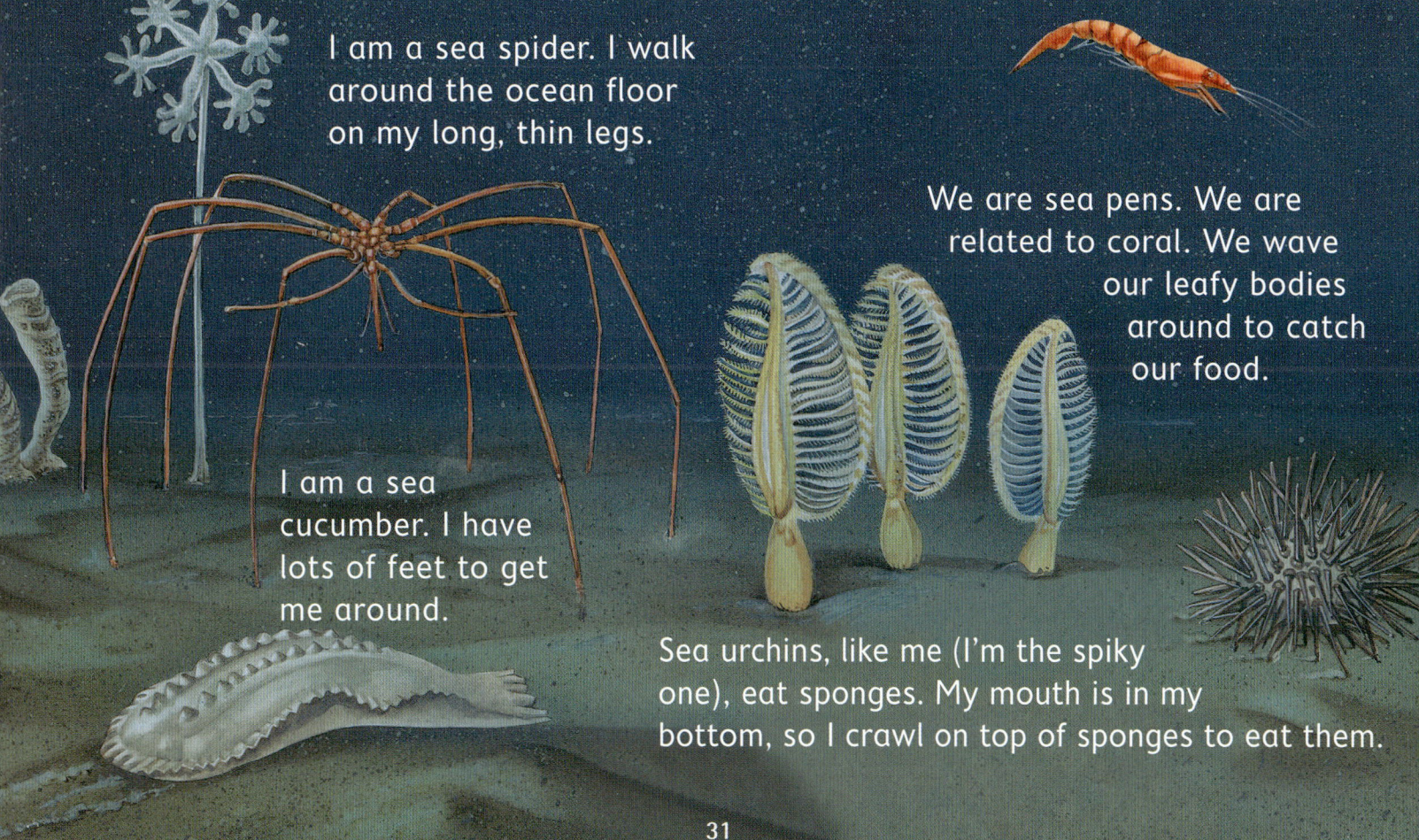

We are giant tube worms. We live close to these strange chimneys on the ocean floor. They are called black smokers. They puff out hot, black jets of water full of goodness for us to live on. We can grow to almost 10 feet (3 m) long.

I am a sea spider. I walk around the ocean floor on my long, thin legs.

We are sea pens. We are related to coral. We wave our leafy bodies around to catch our food.

I am a sea cucumber. I have lots of feet to get me around.

Sea urchins, like me (I'm the spiky one), eat sponges. My mouth is in my bottom, so I crawl on top of sponges to eat them.

Glossary

baleen (buh-LEEN) The bristly plates that hang in the mouths of some whales. They are used to strain food from sea water.

blubber (BLUH-ber) The thick layer of fat some animals that live in cold oceans have.

camouflaged (KA-muh-flahjd) Hidden by colors and marks on an animal's body.

colonies (KAH-luh-neez) Groups of the same type of animals.

krill (KRIL) Small shrimplike animals.

migration (my-GRAY-shun) The movement of animals with the seasons, to find food or to breed.

parasites (PER-uh-syts) Animals or plants that live in or on another animal and are often harmful to it.

polyp (PAH-lip) A tiny animal made up of a stomach, mouth, and tentacles.

predator (PREH-duh-ter) An animal that hunts and kills other animals for food.

zooplankton (zoh-uh-PLANK-ten) Tiny animals that live near the surface of the ocean.

Index

A
albatross 26–27
algae 10, 19
angelfish 11, 13
anglerfish 28
Antarctica 24, 26
Atlantic Ocean 14
Australia 10

B
baleen 22
black smokers 31
boxfish 12

C
camouflage 13, 20
clown fish 12
coral reefs 10–11, 12
cowfish 12

D
defense 12–13
dusky dolphins 20–21

F
firefly squid 29
flying fish 13

G
Great Barrier Reef 10–11
great white shark 4–5
green turtles 14–15
grenadier fish 30
gulper eel 29

H
hammerhead shark 5
hatchetfish 28
humpback whales 22–23

K
kelp 16–17
king penguin 24–25
krill 22

L
lantern fish 28

lobsters 6
loosejaw 29

M
manatees 18–19
migration 14–15
moray eel 11
mullets 13

O
octopus 8–9

P
Pacific Ocean 8
parasites 21, 23
parrotfish 11
polyps 10
porcupine fish 12
Portuguese man-of-war 7

S
scallops 7
sea anemones 6–7, 12
sea cucumbers 30–31

sea horse 11
seals 4–5, 17, 25
sea otters 16–17
sea pens 30–31
sea slug 7
sea spider 31
sea urchins 6–7, 16, 31
sheepshead fish 16
sonar 21
Southern Ocean 26
sponges 11, 30–31
starfish 7, 11
stonefish 12–13

T
tiger shark 5
torpedo ray 13
tripodfish 30
tube worms 31

V
viperfish 28

Z
zooplankton 29

Web Sites

Due to the changing nature of Internet links, PowerKids Press has developed an online list of Web sites related to the subject of this book. This site is updated regularly. Please use this link to access the list: www.powerkidslinks.com/ask/shark/